Built of All I Shape and Name

Built of All I Shape and Name

Poems by

Jessica Genia Simon

Front cover art and design by Davey Levson
@daveylevsonart

ISBN: 978-1-63980-286-9

Kelsay Books
502 South 1040 East, A-119
American Fork, Utah 84003
Kelsaybooks.com

For my family, for my wife, Michelle,
and especially for my grandparents:

Frances Goldman Simon & Richard Lynn Simon
Genia Broclawska Borowski & Moshe Borowski

Acknowledgements

Thank you to the following publications, which published poems in this collection, sometimes in earlier versions and with different titles:

Atlanta Review (Finalist in 2017 International Poetry Competition): "Third Viewing of Two Fridas Philadelphia Museum of Art"

The Edge: "My Birth: A Villanelle"

Slipform 2020 Anthology: "Nightfall at the Pond: A Tritena," "IVF"

Super Stoked: An Anthology of Queer Poetry from the Capturing Fire Slam Fire Slam & Summit: "Third Viewing of Two Fridas Philadelphia Museum of Art"

Tiny Seed Literary Journal: "Vermont House in Winter"

Washington Writers Publishing House, WWPH Writes: "Ocean City Boardwalk" (as "Stuffed Dragons")

Special thank you to Marge Piercy and all the poets at the Marge Piercy Poetry Intensive in June 2022. Thank you to the Glen Echo Writing Group and to Michelle Brafman's Glen Echo writing workshop. Thank you to the DC spoken word community, to Regie Cabico, Lisa Pegram and all the teachers and poets who have helped guide this poet to her current form and this book to its birth.

Thank you to all the members of my family, special gratitude to my spouse, Michelle, for every step of the way.

Contents

Part I

My Birth: A Villanelle

Fast you enter the world so from it you will go.
I am told I was born before the doctor could show.
Will I be so quick to leave? I hope it is not so.

Felt the wind on my tiny face just so.
I was a sensory babe, heard the sparrow, eyed the doe.
Fast you enter the world so from it you will go.

Learned each oohweeoohweeoohweeoh.
The chimes of rain from one leaf to below.
Will I be so quick to leave? I hope it is not so.

I gazed out at the tree from my window.
the seasons; the changes, the winds in the bough.
Fast you enter the world so from it you will go.

They go by quickly; I should know.
Even when I write to catch them and hold.
Will I be so quick to leave? I hope it is not so.

I stare as the afternoon light on the wood floor goes.
I watch it pass up the wall and out the door so I know.
Fast you enter the world so from it you will go.
Will I be so quick to leave? I hope it is not so.

Tree Eyes Looking Down

Schoolyard—Tulip Poplar

They ignore me at their height except to balance a hand on the brown grooves of my skin. They prefer a nearby mulberry bush, its squat bulbous center round and open. They read a copy of *Our Bodies, Ourselves* the boy stole from his sister's bathroom in the hollow of branches next to the jungle gym. They share secrets collected the previous day. The boy says "do it" and laughs. The girl looks at a picture, asks if women start bleeding and never stop. The boy says sex looks like snakes. Years later, the girl will sit on my bulging roots to caress my silent ridges. She will long for the tiny gifts of nectar from swapped honeysuckles stems.

Backyard—White Oak

In the garage, there lies an old hammock. It broke one winter after melted snow soaked it and froze. When the father would sit, it would sag to the ground, but the girl could swing with abandon. She did for years, swatting at the mosquitos or a bee. She hated bugs, but loved me, stared for hours up at my lobed deciduous leaves. At one time, I was a nursery rhyme. Years later, a hideout for a teenage kiss. Then, for a depressed summer, midnight branch silhouettes, black brush strokes across blue light. When she recovered, she saw, as if for the first time, my dark green crown.

Graveyard—American Sycamore

Ten men walk past me with a new box. In it, a woman joins a quarry of dead relatives. The only Jewish cemetery in Norristown, PA. A little girl looks this way and that as if she will fall into one of the geometric beds. Each adult pushes a shovel full of dirt into the hole onto the box. Hunched, they rip small pieces of black cloth pinned to their breasts. Two men turn a crank to lower it. Pulley gears squeak. The girl watches the woman go into the ground. I did not ask to be planted here. I grew despite the visitors who come only to talk to stones. Here, most men lie down, people cry. I shed leaves to cover the rectangles, a gardener rakes them up each winter, others place small rocks on top of vertical stones, prune bushes, leave flowers. Children play hide and seek, teenagers rub against one another, the older ones tend to their ends.

Recurring Dream

The little girl paces
back and forth in a grass meadow
shoulders hunched looking down.

She cannot stop or rest.
Her arms swing as she steps
and turns. She pushes

herself to find the right
flower. The one that will tell her
her how to grow up

the one that will show
her who to love, the one
that will whisper in her ear

she is enough, the one to
teach her how to fill her nose
with what turns towards the sun.

Deck of Cards

I play with the edges of a pad of
       paper, letting them slip by like
a released deck of cards, notice
       a pack near the bread box.

On quiet nights, I write quiet poems.
       I sit in a kitchen and hear
the clock tick, with the porch light off,
       the stove off, everything off.

I fiddle with the loose
       tassels of failed love, stupid fringe,
like the strings I braided on my father's tallit
       as a little girl in temple unsure or bored.

My dad and I used to play gin rummy
       on work nights until I had dates.
I pick up the deck
       and shuffle methodically except

I drop all the cards on the floor.
       I pick up a pen to write a poem
about failed love as if this will
       gather the cards
       untangle the strings
       order the papers
       render the emptiness
anything more than a loss.

Stuffed Prizes

A terrible sweet smell, vinegar French fries
and custard fumes waft down the boardwalk.

The souvenir shops shout trinkets and silkscreen
t-shirts as I watch teenage skinny legs devour
fried dripping funnel cakes and pizza slices.

The Ferris wheel creaks like a rocking chair.
The Jolly Roger, a swoosh of metronomic noise.

Not so long ago, my own small finger would stop and point
at the stuffed prizes (a dragon! a bear!) lined on booth walls.
Dad gave me a dollar to shoot a basket, toss a ring.

The ocean wind would reach out from its giant dark portal
to wave me in and wave me out.

50-Year-Old Dad Teaches 20-Year-Old Daughter How to Bowl

Years ago, my grandfather shined his ball
to place inside a blue leather bowling bag.
It now sits in a dark basement next
to faded trophies.
Dad says *your grandad used to score 185*
every single game.

Now, in the dim fluorescent glow
of this bowling alley, I aim
at a pyramid of pins,
look back, dad grins.
I step forward, onetwothree
twist my wrist, and let go.

Dad clears 150 with three strikes.
I barely break 50. Dad tells me
to use my pointer finger
square my hips,
step together, arm back,
follow through, let go.

Dad tells me I used to heave-ho
between tented legs.
His hair has been feathery white
for as long as I can remember.
We all gray early in this family.

10 turns is all—I hit 5 pins in one go.
Next time, I'm in the gutter.
The ball rolls back through a tunnel of dark.
Spin and spin to hit gutter or pin,
but it all goes dark in the end.
For my dad, I try again.

Even After

On the day she found out she could visit
Eden again on weekends, in her car, alone
it made her believe or want to believe.

She could look left and right
discover clouds unafraid of trees.
The trees were the same trees

that bowed to her, so long ago.
How they had faced her with wet
green sunshine on their backs

and chests, the rays of light
unabashed, the light the way she remembered
it, back before she could shape or name.

She places a hand on her conscious breast
revisits that holy place where each breath
wore the sweet rose scent of purple years.

She turns her head away to the road ahead
reassured that even after the fall
she was allowed a sideways glance to the past.

Fear of Burning

She walked home in a slumber
　　pulled off her boots, shook
　　　　snow from the cuffs
　　　　　　slept one last time as a woman
　　　　　　　　with desires she could deny.

She awoke
　　next to a large window
　　　　saw snowflakes falling, dancing
　　　　　　delicate, floating
　　　　　　　　pieces of sky.

She turned, last night,
　　snow into heat
　　　　allowed her hand to run
　　　　　　from hip to waist to brush
　　　　　　　　the curve of a breast.

She touched lips, kissed a neck,
　　cradled and traced
　　　　hips all the while

　　　　　　shedding nineteen years of learning

　　　　　　not to kiss them for fear of burning.

Part II

Sing, Robin, Sing

A robin sings in winter because he can [. . .],
but he is also in practice for happier times.
                    —Katherine May, Wintering

A robin redbreast perches
on a bare tree branch to sing.
Pit and pat from twig to twig
wind battering his bare talons.

He rides out a windy gust,
hunkers down, beak to bark
flapping warm-blooded feathers
wild to forget the sun as a filmy disk.

Is winter a thing to be endured?
We light candles and small bulbs
to conjure absent flowers,
nudge the sun to come again.

The sky is a gray void
of thin clouds vast and dull.
I poke a head outside the door
only to scurry inside, underneath.

The robin, now fat with scraps,
perches on the deck
puffs his belly, opens his mouth
pushes his hope out in song.

My Mother and the Maple Tree

The old maple tree in the front yard
of my childhood home is half naked
in the early winter chill.

I go home to cover my body with gloves,
socks, slippers, scarves, try to deny
the years that nip at my eyes and hands.

I help my mother pick out books on heart disease
from the library. I know bodies fail. I know they wither
become frail, hunched and shrunken.

Yet the age of a tree shows inside,
rings, growth, girth. An upright trunk with roots
stretched out may still be a tree dying.

Shades of yellow creep up on pinnate leaves,
branches sway, spots of heartwood show
bare through holes along the bark.

My mother sits in a brimmed purple winter hat,
eats a sliced apple. As I watch her pick up
each sweet wedge, I whisper a silent prayer
to the temple of her, for her hidden heart.

Nightfall at the Pond

A Great Blue Heron flaps its pterodactyl wings towards last light.
Outstretched shadows crown the setting sun a tangerine sky.
Reflected trees recede in a slow ebb across the pond.

All human voices quiet, fire smoke lifts, encircles the pond.
Golds to pinks, reds to browns, greens to blue-gray dusk light.
A thick lid of stars covers the blue dome of sky.

Barn swallows rush to their houses aloft to dream of sky.
Bullfrogs groan their deep bass moan across the pond.
Cradle rocks of water lap upon bald cypress trees in moonlight.

At last, the heron vanishes in the sky, beyond the pond into the
deep dark night.

Jewish Tourist in Toledo, Spain

Stones are more reliable than men.
On the walls of this Catholic church,
once a synagogue, then a mosque
a Cross adorns the throne, but a Star of David
hides in a ceiling tile; a Converso.
Arabic appears through whitewash; a Morisco.

In a souvenir shop, a man shows me
a statue of The Virgin Mary
that used to hide a mezuzah
on a door jamb, points to his forearm,
"Jewish blood."

He tells me his grandfather kept
the key to the Toledo home
abandoned after the Inquisition.
A Palestinian man holds onto a key
to his grandfather's house
in Jerusalem, a house that may
or may not, still stand.

There exists a certain amnesia
in countries and pious men.
One God paints over another,
switches the symbol above the door.
Men chisel granite,
build cities atop cities,
say there is nothing beneath,

but stone remains. No matter
how deep truth is buried,
time turns rock
to fossilized braille.

Men hold onto keys
and history flows down
tributaries of memory
to etched stones.
I turn to leave Toledo, cross back
over the bridge as the city ebbs away
through the window of the train.

Why I Studied in Israel for a Year

I went to find you mom.
      in the persimmons, in your cousins, in your friends still
alive in their children, in their memories of you.

I ate salad for breakfast like you said you did,
      I went to the beach where you said you used to go every
weekend and ate chocolate covered banana popsicles.

All these memories I collect from you as an adult,
      I hoard like heirlooms in the hope chest
of my heart.

I relied on a diagram at the granite gravestones
      of your parents, Genia and Moshe,
to help navigate endless rows and columns of Hebrew.

The words all phonetic, unreadable to me.
      like you were for my first 18 years
until I knew to demand answers.

Your childhood was sifted through stolen dreams
      erased history, survivor nightmares, aftermath.
You did not speak child, playful innocence.

You did not speak poetic dreamer, hammock swing.
      I did not speak your mother tongue
or your mother's mother tongue.

You escaped into books when you could, you lived
      near a library and could borrow two at a time.
You read books. I read books. Two different

languages, always language, always seeking
        not just the sound, but meaning. A you are, not just your.
You kept memories from me, tried to protect me.

From what? From you? I searched for you in language.
        I dreamed you, listened for you.
What did your silence mean?

There must be a reason
        you hid devastation in the folds of your heart.
I finally learn.

Your father was alone in a hospital the night before
        the surgeon was scheduled to fix his heart.
He told you to leave, go back to your family

in America, to me, a baby less than one.
        Your thighs barely dry from my birth.
Your father jumped off a balcony

before his heart could be repaired.
        Then you had to bury him.
Your mother already dead from a heart attack,

my brother only three-years-old.
        I did not know until I asked, kept asking.
Your parents used to call you Esther-le.

Your mother, Genia, could not bear
        to hear the German language, she refused
to go back for the restitution money.

Did your parents ever find peace?
            In Poland, in Givataim, in death?
They survived a war to reach Israel.

Yiddish-tinged Hebrew held nightmares
            of dead sisters, brothers, fathers, mothers.
I searched for you, mother.

In black-and-white photos, your long straight dark hair
            frame huge red square plastic-rimmed glasses
a fitted striped sweater and Maxi skirt.

You clutch a folio case of drawings you carry
            door-to-door to find an architecture job in America.
I search in your Carnegie Mellon full scholarship,

in your American Jewish boyfriend, my dad,
            full of boyish enthusiasm, disco and public policy.
You met in a parking lot; he asked if you were Israeli.

Your guilt at leaving your parents in Israel
            hangs like an anvil above your life.
A truth you walk miles around only to reach the start.

You cannot outrun your losses, your griefs.
            You left the country that shaped you, but you shaped me.
I sounded you out, mom, I found you, I'm found.

In Vitro Fertilization

On my belly, a literal dot dot dot,
an ellipsis on either side of my navel.
A stomach speckled with semicolons,
before; after. Perhaps the points
are an embroidery pattern to follow and sew,
or a constellation to trace in the sky.
I take pills that double my breast size,
trick my body into turning mother.

I see the doctor still speaking with charts,
percentages, study x = result y.
I ask another question,
if only to stay a bit longer
in the presence of one pretending
to know, something, anything, for sure.

Human or Avian

With its bone thin talons
untucked, it lay on the
pavement between Clark's
Deli and the Bank of America
building. Untouched.

Ornithologists predict a million
birds die each year flying into
skyscraper windows. They
mistake clear glass for sky.

Its spotted breast is still bright
white, black dots on a downy
brown feather bib, unsullied.

If birds knew of glass, would they
still fly?

This tiny sparrow left me with
no songs, only a still heart and
a soft round head. It lays at
rest, wings limp, beak closed.

Human or avian, we are not made to
fly headfirst into glass.

Bee Sting

A bee stung the finger right above
the wedding ring she put there five years ago.
My first thought was this is a bad omen
could hear my grandmother spit three times
and worry the sting until I forgot the pain.

There I was, tossing crumbs, my sins,
into Rock Creek, for tashlich when it found
me and stung. A friend had just revealed
she was pregnant, due in a few months.
My finger swelled, a pinpointed pain.
I swatted the yellow and black away,
clutched my hand and winced.

My friends opened their purses and pockets
to withdraw pills, ointments, essential oils.
One sees my eyes full of fear, reassures me,
bees make honey, you know.
In other words, pain, but sweetness too.
Months of discomfort will be worth it.

The prods and pricks, what's a little sting?
My first invisible pregnancy lasted
seven weeks. I watched a yolk sac
float on a screen tucked into a thick
uterine lining give way to no heartbeat.
Empty explanations fail
to plug holes that continue to leak.

We speak feverishly of births and abortions,
not all of ways a woman can house
the full span of life and death in between.
The half-lives, the almost weres
she also carries. I run a bit of water
into a dish, mix baking soda into paste
to ease the swollen finger. It, will heal.

Vermont House in Winter

Over and under flows
the brook's water beneath
sheets and jagged edges

of ice. Translucent muffled
rush, the brook spills
over rocks downhill.

A porch wraps around
the house like a scarf
warms a throat.

An Eastern White Pine
stands silent over white snow
now blue in dusk.

An icicle thaws
clear in my fingers.
I pick up a rounded stone

see time smoothed over.
I am the stone, time passes
through me.

When I am gone
the brook will babble on
over stone and hill.

First Miscarriage: A Villanelle

Slow my panting desperate heart.
Dare to wish for blood made kin.
I cling to hope like a lark.

Allow your belly to house a start.
Take a test tube for a spin.
Slow my panting desperate heart.

See the ultrasound fail to spark.
Dig my nails into the skin.
I cling to hope like a lark.

They wheel my gurney into an O.R.
to take out what they had put within.
Slow my desperate panting heart.

If I wait for my womb to restart.
I can try again, again, again.
I cling to hope like the lark.

Unlike a stone thrown in a pond of dark
ripples, I cannot cause a cell to twin.
Slow my panting desperate heart.
I cling to hope like a lark.

Second Miscarriage: Anger Stage of Grief

How inadequate the word miscarriage.
I don't 'miss' the 'carriage.'
I cry at OPB—other people's babies.

A woman asked me
Do you have children? Do you want them?
She clarifies: to carry them?

I muttered to myself, guess not.
My hip bones gave no answer.
Will I have or not? Can I have or not?

Can semen or clots form fetal tissue
and adequate lining, show human growth
hormone on a piss-stained stick?

Should I have shown her my low
AMH score? Perhaps display for her a picture
of my one-time darker line?

Or the ultrasound of normal
sized eggs, get her read of my follicle
length and number

detail my embryonic bags empty of hearts
or rather two hearts that beat for a week
and then stopped.

Third Viewing of "Two Fridas,"
Philadelphia Museum of Art

You worked with organs
because your bones were all
cracked. Look how a vein
sweeps over your shoulder
like a shawl, the heart exists
outside your body like a cloud
you could watch float by.

You hold your own hand,
your organs inside out and flushed,
red wet and beating, the parts
that worked and fed you,
the parts that bleed and love.
What use are bones anyway,
but to house the life that beats between the bars?
Your bars were broken and you beat right
into the mirror, onto the canvas, for all to see,
trivial some would say,
a woman alone in pain paints herself,
trivial, a woman alone in pain,
trivial, a woman alone
with her organs and bones,
alive and beating on pages.

Frida, even as your body
raged, your bones
twisted, your womb
collapsed, you painted for yourself
a dress of stained linen, next to
a more innocent you.
She offered and you took
your own hand, as she pinched
to stop the bleeding
that threatened to end you.

Some Women

Some women I know hold
their pain so deep
the still water will never betray
itself. No breeze will ripple
the surface. Below rocks,
wounds hold ground
buried and bound.

Apology for the "I'm Sorrys"

I apologize for the "I'm sorrys" that escape my mouth in advance of saying almost anything. The apology I give because I am the wrong kind of woman, wrong size, wrong sex. I mean, I am short, squat, my belly protrudes over top my jeans. I apologize for a clitoris that feels pleasure when plucked. I apologize for my speech, I'm sorry for my 'aggressive' tone, meaning louder than you, or meaning too confident, or that I believe in what I am saying. I apologize for my opinions, that I have them in the first place, about most things, that I dare to say them, or argue my rightness, and your wrongness, or speak at all, in a room full of talking men or a room full of quiet women. I apologize for my volume being too brash, for my cackle laugh, for how I am dressed in a sloganed t-shirt and too short mom jeans, or too tight jeans, for my butt not being tight or high enough, for my breasts being different sizes, for the blood falling out of my vagina, for not being dressed up enough. For my hair being too kinky or too curly or straightened or not, for my makeup being applied incorrectly, too little eye liner, too much foundation, not blended in, not enough rouge, or not applied at all, for the hairs on my upper lip which are not blond, for the stain of chocolate ice cream on my pants, for the chip with salsa I just dropped onto the carpet, for the insult that flew too quickly out of my mouth. I apologize in advance before I say what I think. I apologize in case I say what makes you and the room uncomfortable. I apologize for the truth I feel compelled to speak. I apologize to myself for over apologizing. My god, I am so sorry all of the damn time, for what I feel for what I do not feel. How the hell did I learn to give a fuck so often? I am so good at feeling so bad, learned so young to be a good girl, to feel sorry for being bad, being bad is one who does not follow rules. I follow them. What, in a day full of apologies, can an apology even mean?

Make Me like the Crocus, the Daffodil, the Cherry Blossom

I wish to be open like the crocus,
first in spring in the right sun and temperature.
Or, no, I wish to be more like the daffodil,
she may wilt briefly, a curtsy before the big reveal,
but on a cold spring day, she is canary yellow collar
encircled trumpet, full-throated, upright, proud.
I'll be like that. Or no, I'll be like the cherry blossoms,
yes, they have it right, they do not open
until ready. Buds first, red and plucky.
Overnight, they bust out pink pom poms
like little cheerleaders or firework clusters,
pink and white for a week or two, then to lush green.

But here I stand, bent over the bathroom sink
naked, head in my hands, in front of a shower
fogged mirror, a lavender mud mask smeared
across my face to rinse away toxins.
I hope to drain myself of sorrow and dead things,
empty myself of any blood I do not need
anything that does not live or help me live
unsheath my body of unnecessary skin,
shed what I can to be new, new as I can be now,
with decades done.

Free me of all coats, cloaks, coverings,
Free me of all pouches or pockets,
Free me of hidden things, of secrets,
Free me of sandbags of worry pressed against future floods,
Free me from the future, the past, from expectation,
Free me from shoulds, from woulds, from perfection,
Free me from visions of could-have-beens, would-have-beens,
Free me of any tense but the present,
Free me, dammit, from physical time,
Free me of any and all I do not need.

Make me like the crocus, the daffodil, the cherry blossom.

Built of All I Shape and Name

The gifts my mother gave me:
books on shelves, a garden watered.
These are treasures, but just as worthy,
was the dirt beneath.
The gift my mother tried to give me,
her American child, was silence.
My mother tried to bury
her fears, but at thirty-eight,
I prune and tend these lush, leafy
potted plants,
smelling of girlhood dreams.
I sit content in my own home
built of all I shape and name.

Born to Holocaust survivor parents
who re-lived their deaths over and over
after fascism failed to kill them,
these parents urged my mother to be
a dutiful daughter, warned
her not to marry for love,
but whomever will have you first.
Unsaid: those you love too easily die.
Do not swim or ride a bike.
Life is not amusement.
For them, clouds were not clouds,
but smoke.

Instead, my mother finished
her tests first with perfect scores,
took the full scholarship
to Pittsburgh, PA, moved
to a new home, fell in love
with my American father
and architecture, built stability
out of steel beams

and concrete foundation.
On a basement drafting table,
my mother finds her instruments:
pencil, compass, three-sided ruler.
My mother architect designs strong
solid structures that withstand.

Perhaps my mother thought silence
could stop the flow of fear
to her womb.

For years, it worked.
I slept peaceful sleep, wrote
poems to birds chirping in treetops
believed my arms, wings, ready to fly.
I could not fall.
Until I did.

My own nest took many years to build,
decades to weave together the question
I needed to ask and answer.
Why did my skin crawl with fear?
I carried carefully chosen twigs
of inexplicable superstitions
in my maw, found colorful scraps
crawling on hands and knees
amidst weeds, pricked
my fingers on evergreen blades
hidden in the dead of winter,
observed the dandelion
in a sidewalk crack,
stepped on hundreds of times,
grow.

About the Author

Jessica Genia Simon began writing poetry at age seven. As a teenager, she attended the University of Virginia's Young Writers Workshop, competed and won a spot on the Brave New Voices 2001 D.C. National Youth Poetry Slam Team. She earned a B.A. in English and Textual Studies and Policy Studies at Syracuse University and her M.S. in Education from University of Pennsylvania. She spent a year in Jerusalem, Israel, studying at Pardes Institute for Jewish Studies, and volunteering with LGBTQ+ and middle east peace organizations. She works at a gun violence prevention nonprofit in D.C. and lives with her wife, daughter, and orange short-haired tabby cat, Zahav, in Silver Spring, Maryland. This is her first poetry collection.

ᙡᏉ

www.ingramcontent.com/pod-product-compliance
Lightning Source LLC
Chambersburg PA
CBHW051811090426
42737CB00036B/2970